THE SPOTS THAT DEFINE ME

A VITILIGO JOURNEY

ROSHAAN NARKEDAYY

To all those who have ever felt like they didn't quite fit in.

This book is dedicated to you.

May it remind you that your differences are what make you unique and beautiful, and that there is nothing wrong with being who you are.

May it inspire you to love and accept yourself, and to never give up on your dreams.

And may it serve as a reminder that you are not alone. There is a community of people out there who understand and support you, and who will always be there for you no matter what.

With love and solidarity,

Roshaan Narkedayy

Contents

Foreword

As a Public Health Professional, I have seen many patients with Vitiligo over the years. I have witnessed firsthand the physical and emotional toll that this condition can take on a person.

But I have also seen something else: the incredible resilience and strength of those who have Vitiligo. I have seen people who have been stigmatized and discriminated against because of their skin, yet who have refused to let it define them. I have seen people who have turned their condition into a source of pride, and who have used their experiences to advocate for others.

That's why I was so moved when Roshaan approached me about writing this book. I knew that his story would be a powerful one, and I was not disappointed.

In these pages, Roshaan shares her journey with Vitiligo in all its complexities. He doesn't shy away from the difficult moments or the painful memories, but He also doesn't let them overshadow the moments of triumph and joy.

What struck me most about this book, though, was Roshaan's courage. It takes a lot of courage to be vulnerable, to share our stories with the world, and to advocate for change. And yet, that's exactly what he has done.

I believe that this book will be an inspiration to anyone who has ever felt like they didn't quite fit in. It will remind us that our differences are what make us beautiful, and that there is power in embracing who we are.

Thank you, Roshaan Narkedayy, for sharing your story with us. May it inspire us all to be more accepting, more compassionate, and more resilient.

Dr. Kiran Narkhede
Technical Consultant, World bank

Preface

I never thought that I would write a book about my journey with Vitiligo. In fact, for many years, I didn't even want to talk about it.

Growing up, I was ashamed of my skin. Although i know my father who had Vitiligo, and I didn't understand why my skin was different from everyone else's. I was bullied and teased, and I often felt like I didn't belong.

It wasn't until I was older that I started to realize that my skin was just one part of who I am. I started to see that there was nothing wrong with being different, and that my differences were what made me unique.

But even then, I still struggled with the emotional impact of Vitiligo. I still felt self-conscious when people stared at me, and I still felt frustrated when doctors couldn't offer me a cure.

It wasn't until I started to connect with other people who had Vitiligo that I truly started to heal. I found a community of people who understood what I was going through, who didn't judge me for my skin, and who celebrated my differences.

And that's what inspired me to write this book. I wanted to share my story with others who might be going through something similar. I wanted to offer hope to those who feel alone, and to remind them that they are not the only ones.

This book is not just about my journey with Vitiligo. It's about the power of community, the importance of self-acceptance, and the beauty of diversity. It's about finding strength in our differences, and about using our experiences to create a better world for all.

I hope that this book will inspire you to embrace your own differences, to stand up for what you believe in, and to never give up on your dreams.

With love,

Roshaan Narkedayy

Acknowledgements

Writing this book has been an incredible journey, and I couldn't have done it without the support and encouragement of so many people. To each and every one of you, thank you.

First and foremost, I want to thank my family for always being there for me, even when things were tough. Your love and support have been my rock throughout this journey, and I couldn't have done it without you.

To my friends and fellow Vitiligo warriors, thank you for sharing your stories with me, for listening to mine, and for reminding me that I am never alone. Your strength and resilience inspire me every day.

To the team at Notion Press, thank you for believing in this book and for helping to bring it to life. Your hard work and dedication are truly appreciated.

Finally, to everyone who has ever shown me kindness, compassion, and understanding, thank you. Whether it was a stranger on the street who smiled at me, a friend who gave me a shoulder to cry on, or a fellow Vitiligo warrior who shared their story with me, your kindness has made all the difference.

This book is dedicated to all of you. Thank you for being a part of my journey.

Introduction

What is Vitiligo?

Vitiligo is a condition that causes the loss of pigmentation in the skin, resulting in white patches or spots. The exact cause of Vitiligo is not fully understood, but it is thought to be an autoimmune disorder, in which the body's immune system attacks and destroys the melanocytes, the cells responsible for producing pigment in the skin.

Vitiligo can affect any part of the body, but it most commonly appears on the face, hands, feet, and other areas that are exposed to the sun. The patches can vary in size and shape, and they often spread over time.

While Vitiligo is not a life-threatening condition, it can have a significant impact on a person's quality of life. The loss of pigmentation can be particularly noticeable in people with darker skin tones, and the psychological impact of Vitiligo can be significant.

Many people with Vitiligo report feeling self-conscious or embarrassed about their skin, and they may experience anxiety or depression as a result.

White patches on My Hands

There is no known cure for Vitiligo, but there are treatments that can help to reduce the appearance of the white patches. These include topical medications, phototherapy, sand in some cases, surgical procedures. Additionally, there are a number of support groups and organizations that offer resources and information for people living with Vitiligo.

My personal experience with Vitiligo

Living with Vitiligo can be challenging, both physically and emotionally. For me, the first signs of Vitiligo appeared when I was in my early twenties, with small white patches appearing on my face. At first, I didn't think much of it, but as the patches grew larger and more noticeable, I became increasingly self-conscious.

I found myself avoiding social situations and covering up my skin whenever possible, even in hot weather. I felt like everyone was staring at me, and I became obsessed with finding ways to hide my patches.

Over time, I learned to accept my condition and to embrace my unique appearance. I started connecting with other people who had Vitiligo, and I found strength in our shared experiences. I also learned about different treatments that could help reduce the appearance of the white patches.

Now, while I still have moments of self-consciousness, I am more confident and comfortable in my own skin. I have learned to love and accept myself, patches and all, and I am proud to share my story in the hope of helping others who may be struggling with Vitiligo.

My journey with Vitiligo has been challenging, but it has also taught me a lot about resilience, self-acceptance, and the power of community.

CHAPTER TWO

The Early Years

I never imagined that a skin condition would end up shaping so much of my life, but that's the thing about Vitiligo - it's unpredictable and all-consuming. Looking back, I can see how the first signs of it were there, even though I didn't fully understand what was happening at the time.

As a child, seeing my father's Vitiligo was a confusing and unsettling experience for me. I didn't understand why his skin had white patches, and I was afraid to ask. I remember feeling like it was something to be ashamed of, and I didn't want anyone else to know.

Over time, as I grew older and learned more about Vitiligo, I began to understand that it was a harmless condition and nothing to be ashamed of. I learned to see my father's patches as a unique aspect of his appearance, and I grew to love and accept him just the way he was.

In many ways, my father's Vitiligo has been a source of strength and inspiration for me. He has always been open about his condition and willing to talk about it, even when others were uncomfortable or judgmental. He has taught me about resilience, self-acceptance, and the importance of embracing our differences.

While I would never wish Vitiligo on anyone, I am grateful for the lessons that my father's experience has taught me. He has shown me that we can find beauty in our imperfections and that our differences make us unique and special.

As I entered my teenage years, the spots became more noticeable, and I began to feel increasingly self-conscious. I remember trying to cover them up with makeup or self-tanner, but nothing seemed to work. I started to avoid social situations and became more withdrawn, spending most of my time alone.

Looking back, I realize how much the early signs of Vitiligo affected me. They were the first indication that my life would be different from what I had imagined, and I wasn't sure how to handle it. But even in those early years, I can see the seeds of resilience and determination that would later help me face the challenges that lay ahead.

Coping with the emotional impact

Coping with the emotional impact of Vitiligo can be a difficult and ongoing process. Many people with Vitiligo struggle with feelings of self-consciousness, shame, and anxiety, especially in the early stages of their diagnosis. It can be challenging to come to terms with the fact that your appearance is changing in a way that you have no control over.

One of the most important things that you can do to cope with the emotional impact of Vitiligo is to talk about your feelings with someone you trust. This might be a close friend or family member, a therapist, or a support group of others who have Vitiligo. Sharing your experiences and feelings can help you feel less alone and more understood.

It's also important to focus on self-care and self-compassion. This might include practicing mindfulness or meditation, engaging in activities that bring you joy and relaxation, or treating yourself to small acts of self-kindness, such as taking a relaxing bath or enjoying a favorite treat.

Another helpful coping strategy is to educate yourself about Vitiligo and the different treatment options that are available. This can help you feel more empowered and in control of your situation. It's important to remember that while there is no cure for Vitiligo, there are treatments that can help reduce the appearance of white patches and improve overall skin health.

Overall, coping with the emotional impact of Vitiligo is an ongoing process that requires patience, self-compassion, and a willingness to reach out for support when needed. With time and self-care, it is possible to find peace and acceptance in your unique appearance.

CHAPTER THREE

Living with Vitiligo

Living with Vitiligo has taught me that people can be incredibly cruel and judgmental. Despite the fact that it's a harmless skin condition, there is a lot of stigma and misunderstanding surrounding Vitiligo.

I remember the first time I heard someone whispering about my spots. It was in the school cafeteria, and I overheard a group of girls talking about how "gross" my skin looked. I tried to ignore them and focus on my lunch, but their words stung. It was the first time I realized that my skin was going to be a constant source of scrutiny and judgment.

Over the years, I've had countless experiences of people staring, whispering, or making insensitive comments about my skin. It's hard not to let those comments get to you, and for a long time, I let them define how I felt about myself.

But as I got older, I started to realize that the problem wasn't with my skin - it was with other people's attitudes. I began to speak out against Vitiligo stigma and to educate others about the condition. I started volunteering at local support groups and participating in awareness campaigns.

While it's still difficult to deal with the stigma of Vitiligo, I've learned that by speaking out and advocating for myself and others, I can make a difference. I've also discovered a strong community of people with Vitiligo, who understand the challenges that come with living with this condition.

Living with Vitiligo in India

Living with Vitiligo in India can be challenging due to cultural beliefs and stigmas surrounding the condition. Many people in India believe that Vitiligo is a curse or punishment, and there is a lack of awareness about the medical causes and treatment options available. This can lead to a great deal of discrimination and social isolation for people living with Vitiligo.

In addition, many people in India are deeply invested in traditional beauty standards that prioritize fair skin. This can make it even more difficult for individuals with Vitiligo to feel accepted and valued in their communities.

Despite these challenges, there are many people in India who are working to raise awareness about Vitiligo and promote acceptance and understanding. There are support groups and advocacy organizations that offer resources and support to individuals living with Vitiligo and their families.

It's also important to note that there are many successful and accomplished individuals in India who have Vitiligo, including celebrities and public figures who are using their platform to raise awareness and promote acceptance.

Social stigma

Social stigma related to appearance in marriage is still prevalent in many parts of India, particularly in arranged marriages. Vitiligo, being a visible skin condition, can be a significant source of stigma and discrimination in the marriage market.

In many Indian communities, fair skin is considered a desirable trait for a bride or groom. The perception that Vitiligo is a disfiguring skin condition that affects one's appearance can lead to individuals with the condition being rejected as potential partners.

Furthermore, the belief that Vitiligo is contagious or hereditary can also contribute to the social stigma surrounding the condition. This can result in individuals with Vitiligo being ostracized from their communities or being subject to discriminatory practices.

To combat this stigma, there are many organizations and individuals working to raise awareness about Vitiligo and promote acceptance and inclusion. Advocacy groups and support networks provide resources and guidance for individuals and families affected by Vitiligo, and they also work to challenge harmful stereotypes and misinformation.

While social stigma related to Vitiligo in marriage and appearance remains a challenge in India, there is hope for change through education, advocacy, and community building.

The Uncomfortable Stares

In social situations, when I entered a room, people would stare at the patches on my skin. It felt like they were intensely curious about my appearance, but not in a good way.

Their eyes would stay on me, making me feel uncomfortable and exposed. It seemed like they were examining and judging how I looked. Each stare invaded my privacy and personal space, leaving me feeling self-conscious and inadequate.

I just wanted to feel normal and be seen for who I truly am, beyond the way I looked. But their stares made me doubt myself and my worth. It was a daily struggle to remind myself that my value goes beyond my physical appearance.

The stares came in different forms: whispered conversations, quick glances, and open stares that made me feel like I was being closely examined. Some people seemed curious, while others looked at me with pity or even dislike. It was clear that my vitiligo made me stand out, but it also made me feel like I didn't fit into society's idea of beauty.

Those stares reflected the misunderstandings and ignorance about vitiligo. Many people hadn't encountered someone with this condition before, so they didn't know how to react. Instead of trying to understand or engage in a conversation, they chose to stare, keeping their distance and making me feel uncomfortable.

With time, I realized that their stares didn't define my worth. They were more about their own insecurities and limited perspectives. Understanding this helped me detach myself from their opinions and embrace my uniqueness.

I found strength in those uncomfortable stares. They pushed me to challenge society's expectations and break free from the limitations that held me back. I stood tall, refusing to let their stares diminish my self-worth.

In the midst of those stares, I found comfort and support from my friends and family. They saw beyond my appearance, accepting and loving me for who I am. Their unwavering support gave me the courage to rise above the judgment and reclaim my confidence.

I learned the power of self-acceptance. I began to appreciate myself, flaws and all, understanding that my vitiligo was not a flaw but a unique part of me. I embraced the beauty in my differences and realized that true acceptance starts from within.

As I continued to navigate social settings, the stares remained a part of my journey, but their impact gradually lessened. I focused on building genuine connections, engaging in meaningful conversations that went beyond appearances. I met people who looked past the surface and appreciated the essence of who I am.

I became an advocate for awareness and education. I wanted to dispel the ignorance surrounding vitiligo and promote empathy and understanding. Through sharing my experiences and having open conversations, I hoped to inspire others to see beyond appearances and embrace the diversity that makes our world beautiful.

Today, as I move through social interactions, I stand tall, unaffected by the uncomfortable stares. I have found strength within myself and cultivated a deep sense of self-acceptance.

The stares may still come, but they no longer have power over me. Instead, I proudly wear my vitiligo as a part of who I am, confident in my own skin.

Relationships & Vitiligo

Vitiligo can have a significant impact on an individual's relationships, including friendships, romantic partnerships, and familial relationships. The condition's visible symptoms can contribute to feelings of self-consciousness and anxiety, making it challenging to form and maintain healthy relationships.

For individuals with Vitiligo who are dating, disclosing the condition to a potential partner can be a difficult decision. Fear of rejection or discrimination can lead to feelings of vulnerability and anxiety. However, disclosing the condition early on can also help to build trust and foster understanding within the relationship.

Familial relationships can also be affected by Vitiligo. Family members may struggle to understand the condition and its impact on their loved one, leading to misunderstandings and strained relationships. Support and education for family members can help to promote understanding and foster a more supportive environment.

In addition, support groups and online communities can be valuable resources for individuals with Vitiligo seeking to connect with others who understand their experiences. These communities can provide a sense of belonging, validation, and support, which can be essential for maintaining healthy relationships.

From the moment I was diagnosed with vitiligo, my parents' worry became a prominent presence in my life. They watched as patches of pigmentation vanished from my skin, their hearts heavy with concern and unanswered questions. Their love for me remained unwavering, but I could sense their worry, their fear of how the world would perceive me.

Parenting & Vitiligo

Parenting can present unique challenges for individuals with Vitiligo. For parents with Vitiligo, raising children with vitiligo can be an even greater obstacle, as they may face additional concerns about how their condition may affect their children's development and well-being.

Very Important here is Parents can support their kids through a vitiligo diagnosis.

Educate themselves and their children about the condition:

Understanding what vitiligo is, how it develops, and how it affects the body can help parents and their children cope with the diagnosis. Parents can also provide information about treatment options and ways to manage the condition.

Foster a positive self-image:

Parents can help their children build a positive self-image by encouraging them to focus on their strengths and talents, rather than their appearance. Parents can also help their children develop coping mechanisms to deal with any negative comments or bullying related to their condition.

Encourage healthy habits:

A healthy lifestyle can help manage the symptoms of vitiligo. Parents can encourage their children to eat a balanced diet, get regular exercise, and protect their skin from the sun.

Seek support:

Parents and children with vitiligo can benefit from joining support groups or seeking out a therapist who can help them cope with any emotional challenges related to the condition.

Foster open communication:

Encouraging open and honest communication can help children feel comfortable talking about their condition with their parents. Parents can also encourage their children to express their feelings and provide a supportive environment to talk about any challenges they may be facing.

Dating & Vitiligo

Dating with Vitiligo can present unique challenges, as the condition can affect an individual's self-esteem and confidence. However, it's important to remember that Vitiligo does not define a person and that there are many people who are accepting of differences in others.

No matter how much we deny it, but many vitiligo fighters associate their self-worth with their relationship, which only makes it crucial for their first date to go well.

It's important to remember that Vitiligo does not define one's worth as a person, and that the right person will appreciate and accept them for who they are, including any physical differences.

While it's understandable to feel nervous or anxious about a first date, it's important to focus on being confident in oneself and presenting oneself authentically. It may also be helpful to discuss Vitiligo with the other person early on in the relationship, in order to address any concerns or questions they may have and establish open communication.

Everyone has their own preferences and priorities when it comes to relationships, and it's not always a reflection of one's worth or attractiveness as a person.

Moving on from a relationship where Vitiligo was a factor was challenging for me, but it's important to prioritize one's own well-being and happiness.

It was a painful reminder that not everyone would understand or accept my journey.

CHAPTER FIVE

Emotional Health

"**Embrace your differences, seek support, express yourself creatively, and never let vitiligo hold you back from pursuing your dreams.**"

Vitiligo can have a significant impact on an individual's emotional health. I experienced feelings of self-consciousness, shame, and anxiety related to self appearance. The unpredictable nature of the condition, as well as the social stigma surrounding it, can also lead to feelings of isolation and loneliness.

Over the time I realised that it is important for me to prioritize self emotional well-being and seek out support when needed. This may involve speaking with a therapist or counselor who specializes in treating individuals with chronic skin conditions, joining a support group for people with Vitiligo, or seeking out trusted friends and family members to talk to.

Practicing self-care is also essential for managing emotional health with Vitiligo. This may include activities like **meditation, exercise, spending time** in nature, or engaging in hobbies and interests that bring joy and fulfillment. This all help me a lot !!

It's important to remember that Vitiligo does not define a person's worth or identity, and that there are many people in the world who will appreciate and accept them for who they are, Vitiligo and all. By prioritizing emotional health and self-care, individuals with Vitiligo can lead fulfilling and meaningful lives.

Managing Post-Traumatic Stress

Managing post-traumatic stress in people with Vitiligo involves a multifaceted approach that includes therapy, medication, and self-care techniques. Therapy can be helpful in addressing the underlying emotional issues related to the trauma, such as feelings of shame, guilt, and anxiety.

Seek professional help

It is an important step in managing post-traumatic stress in people with Vitiligo. A therapist or counselor who specializes in treating individuals with PTSD can provide the necessary support and guidance to help individuals work through their emotional issues and develop coping strategies to manage their symptoms.

Practice self-care, Meditation

Self-care involves taking intentional actions to care for your physical, emotional, and mental well-being. This can include activities such as exercise, healthy eating, getting enough sleep, and engaging in hobbies and activities that bring you joy.

Meditation is a practice that involves training your mind to focus and achieve a state of calmness and relaxation. It can be helpful in reducing stress and anxiety, improving mental clarity and focus, and promoting a sense of well-being.

Connect

Connecting with others who have Vitiligo through support groups or online communities. Engaging in creative activities, such as painting, drawing, or writing. Practicing mindfulness, such as taking time to be present in the moment and focusing on your senses

Avoid exposure to triggers

Triggers are specific events, situations, or experiences that can cause emotional distress and can worsen symptoms of post-traumatic stress.

Some common triggers for people with Vitiligo may include:

- Social situations where their appearance may be scrutinized or judged
- Negative comments or experiences related to their skin condition
- Stressful life events or situations that can exacerbate symptoms

Cognitive behavioral therapy

It is a form of therapy that can be effective in managing post-traumatic stress in people with Vitiligo.

In CBT, individuals work with a therapist to identify and challenge negative or distorted thoughts related to their Vitiligo and the traumatic experiences associated with it. Through this process, they can develop more adaptive ways of thinking that promote self-esteem and reduce emotional distress.

CBT can also involve the use of behavioral techniques, such as exposure therapy, which involves gradually exposing the individual to situations that trigger anxiety or distress related to their Vitiligo. Through repeated exposure and the use of relaxation techniques, individuals can learn to manage their anxiety and reduce the impact of post-traumatic stress on their emotional well-being.

How I deal comments

People with vitiligo often face insulting comments about their skin condition. It can be hard to deal with such situations, but there are ways to respond in a calm and effective way.

- People may make fun of you because they don't understand vitiligo or are insecure themselves. Don't let them get the satisfaction of seeing you upset.
- Tell the person how you feel and how their comments affect your relationship.
- Sometimes, ignoring the insult is the best response, as it shows that you're not affected by it.
- If someone is making fun of you, you can try to turn the joke back on them in a lighthearted way.
- Document things you like about yourself to remind you that you are beautiful and strong.
- Doing things that make you feel good can help boost your self-esteem.
- If the comments are abusive or derogatory, report it to the appropriate authorities.

Stepping into the job interview room, my heart raced with a blend of excitement and trepidation. As I sat across from the interviewer, I couldn't help but notice their curious glances darting towards the patches of depigmentation on my skin. The silence in the room felt suffocating, and my palms grew clammy as I awaited their first question.

As the interview proceeded, I couldn't shake the nagging thought that my vitiligo might overshadow my qualifications and skills. Would they perceive me as less capable or less professional? Doubt crept into my mind, and it took all my strength to maintain composure and confidence.

Behind my forced smile, I battled the fear of judgment. Would they view my vitiligo as a weakness or a hindrance? I yearned for an equal opportunity to showcase my abilities without the shadow of prejudice casting doubt upon me. Yet, in that moment, I had little control over how others would perceive me.

I mustered my courage, relying on my expertise and preparation to navigate the questions with precision. I spoke with passion, my words flowing smoothly despite the unease that threatened to engulf me. Deep down, I wished to be evaluated solely on the merits of my qualifications, my dedication, and my potential to contribute to the organization.

The interviewer's gaze lingered on my vitiligo for a fraction of a second longer than necessary, and I felt a surge of vulnerability. I reminded myself that my skin did not define my abilities or my worth. I had fought battles within myself, overcoming self-doubt and societal prejudice, to reach this moment. I had cultivated resilience and determination in the face of adversity, and those qualities were far more important than any superficial judgment.

In that pivotal interview, I decided to embrace my uniqueness. I presented my accomplishments with confidence, highlighting my skills and experiences, proving that I was a capable candidate beyond the confines of my appearance. I hoped the interviewer would see past the patches on my skin and recognize the value I could bring to their organization.

After what felt like an eternity, the interview concluded. As I left the room, a mix of emotions coursed through me—relief, anticipation, and a glimmer of hope. The outcome remained uncertain, but regardless of the result, I knew that I had shown up as my authentic self, undeterred by the challenges posed by my vitiligo.

With each interview, I grew stronger. I learned to face the world head-on, unapologetic for the canvas of my skin. While the fear of judgment still lingered, I held onto the belief that my worth extended far beyond physical appearances. I vowed to continue pursuing opportunities, knowing that the right organization would recognize my potential, appreciating the diversity I brought to the table.

As I walked away from that interview, I carried with me a newfound determination to shatter the confines of societal expectations. My journey with vitiligo had taught me that my value as an individual lay not in the uniformity of my appearance but in the strength of my character and the depth of my abilities.

CHAPTER SIX

Proudly Spotted

My Vitiligo story starts when I first noticed a very tiny but persistent white patch appearing on my neck after I cut my long Mahendra Singh Dhoni Style hairs in 2008.

At first, I didn't know what to make of it. But as the patches began to spread, I realized that I had vitiligo, a condition that causes loss of skin pigmentation.

I remember feeling heartbroken at my hostel when I first learned about the condition through my doctor brother, as I was worried about how it would affect my looks as I aged.

I cried myself to sleep that night, alone on a summer vacation at my hostel in the evening, before calling my parents and friends to share the news.

In the next few months, I felt self-conscious around classmates & people, whether on the bus, at college functions, or while shopping malls. However, I quickly realized that my father already had the same condition for 90% of the body, and that the appearance of the white patches was not as noticeable till my young age as I had feared.

As a young living with vitiligo, I faced a lot of discrimination and misunderstanding. People would stare at me or make rude comments, as if my skin condition made me less of a person. It was a difficult time, and I often felt ashamed of my appearance.

I often refer to myself as **"Proudly Spotted,"** and I view this condition as a blessing rather than curse. I came to understand that my differences were something to be celebrated, not hidden.

I learned to love myself for who I was, and to stand up against discrimination and prejudice. It has helped me see things from a new perspective and focus on things that actually matter. It has also helped me filter out shallow people who only bring me down and appreciate the beauty of diversity.

But over time,. I wanted to spread positivity and appreciation among the vitiligo community, so I started to connect with others who had the condition, both online and offline. Through social media platforms, I inspired others to embrace their own differences and feel confident in their skin. I also collaborated with other creators in the vitiligo community to spread awareness and positivity.

While I appreciated the concern and support from others over the time, I also faced questions and unwanted attention about my condition in public places. Many people asked me about the various treatments available for vitiligo, not realizing the sensitivity of the topic. It was important for me to challenge misconceptions and educate others about vitiligo treatment, while also respecting boundaries and the sensitivity of the topic.

My newfound confidence didn't come overnight, Unfortunately, my journey wasn't always easy. Despite my newfound confidence and self-love, I still faced discrimination and offensive comments from some people regarding relationships, marriage.

In particular, when I started to look for a job after finishing college, I faced discrimination from potential employers.

Some interviewers would make distasteful comments about my skin condition, questioning my ability to perform the job. I found it frustrating and disheartening that some people couldn't look past my appearance and see the capable person I was.

But I didn't let these experiences hold me back. I knew that I deserved respect and equal treatment, and I continued to apply for jobs and pursue my dreams.

Eventually, I landed a few jobs at a company that valued diversity and inclusivity. Also found a life partner that she wants me in her life despite all these situations. I felt welcomed and appreciated for my skills and abilities, rather than judged for my appearance.

This experience taught him the importance of advocating for oneself and standing up against discrimination, and I continued to use my own as a platform to make a positive difference in the world.

My vitiligo journey is a testament to the power of self-acceptance & community. With positivity, self-love, & determination, anything is possible. I hope, I can inspire others with vitiligo to embrace their differences, seek support, express themselves creatively, and never let their condition hold them back from pursuing their dreams.

" I accept myself as I am "

Communicate and Connect

I had the pleasure of meeting Aastha Shah, Digital creator at Techsparks Mumbai 2023, and let me tell you, she is even more amazing in person!

Aastha's story of embracing her skin and breaking down beauty standards is truly empowering. Her unique style and positive energy radiate through her content, and she is truly changing the game in the fashion industry.

Lessons that inspires me

I learned a lot from Aastha and was inspired by her creativity, dedication, and passion for her work.

- **Embrace your uniqueness:**

Aastha emphasized the importance of embracing your uniqueness and not trying to conform to what others expect of you. She explained how she found success by staying true to her own creative vision and being authentic in her work.

As creatives, we all have something unique to offer, and it's important to embrace that and let it shine through in our work.

- **Focus on the process:**

Aastha stressed the importance of focusing on the creative process rather than just the end result. She explained how she enjoys the journey of creating, and how it's important to enjoy the process and not just the finished product.

This mindset can help us stay motivated and inspired even when facing creative blocks or setbacks.

- **Stay true to your values:**

Finally, Aastha talked about the importance of staying true to your values and using your work to make a positive impact in the world.

She explained how she uses her platform to promote social causes and make a difference in people's lives.

As spotted by vitiligo (skin condition) at a young age, it turn out to be blessing in disguise, helped her learn to accept herself and become more confident.

Her message of self-love and acceptance is exactly what we need in today's world.

Seeing Aastha's confidence and positive attitude has also motivated me to work on my own self-talk and to approach challenges with a growth mindset.

Celebrating Our Differences

My journey with Vitiligo has been filled with challenges, but it's also been a journey of self-discovery and growth. I've learned to love and accept myself, spots and all, and I've come to appreciate the unique beauty that comes with being different.

Through my experiences, I've also learned that there's a lot of work to be done when it comes to Vitiligo awareness and acceptance. There are still so many people who don't understand the condition, and who stigmatize those who have it.

But I'm hopeful that things are changing. There are more and more people speaking out about Vitiligo, and more and more resources available for those who are struggling with it.

My hope is that by sharing my story and advocating for Vitiligo awareness and acceptance, I can help create a world that's more understanding and compassionate. I believe that everyone deserves to be celebrated for who they are, regardless of the color of their skin or the spots on it.

So let's continue to celebrate our differences, and let's work towards a future that's more inclusive and accepting for all. With love, acceptance, and understanding, we can make a real difference in the world.

Today, I stand tall, no longer defined by my vitiligo but enriched by the lessons it has taught me. My journey has shaped me into a resilient individual, capable of embracing both the light and dark shades of life.

Vitiligo, once perceived as an obstacle, has become a catalyst for my personal and emotional growth. It has pushed me to challenge societal norms, to question the narrow definitions of beauty, and to embrace the richness of diversity in all its forms. Through the ups and downs, I have come to understand that our true worth lies not in the uniformity of our appearance, but in the authenticity of our hearts and the contributions we make to the world.

Along the way, I have encountered my better half Radhika, who have seen beyond the surface, who have recognized the beauty in our differences, and who have embraced me wholeheartedly. Her love and acceptance have been invaluable in shaping my self-perception and building my confidence.

With her support, I have learned to celebrate my unique canvas, knowing that my worth is not diminished by the absence of pigmentation, but rather enriched by the vibrant colors that define me.

Valuable sources

Vitiligo Support and Research Foundation (VSRF) - The VSRF website provides comprehensive information about vitiligo, including causes, symptoms, treatments, and research updates. They also offer support resources and connect individuals through forums and support groups. *(Website: www.vitiligosupport.org)*

National Vitiligo Foundation (NVF) - The NVF website offers a wide range of resources for individuals with vitiligo, including educational materials, treatment options, and support networks. They also organize events and campaigns to raise awareness and promote understanding of the condition. *(Website: www.nvfi.org)*

Vitiligo Society - The Vitiligo Society website serves as a valuable resource for individuals seeking information about vitiligo. It provides details on research, treatment options, and personal stories. They also offer support groups and host events to bring together those affected by vitiligo. *(Website: www.vitiligosociety.org.uk)*

American Vitiligo Research Foundation (AVRF) - The AVRF website focuses on raising awareness about vitiligo and funding research initiatives. It offers information about the condition, treatment options, and support resources for individuals and families. *(Website: www.avrf.org)*

World Vitiligo Day - World Vitiligo Day is a global campaign dedicated to raising awareness about vitiligo. Their website provides educational materials, personal stories, and information about events and initiatives happening worldwide. *(Website: www.worldvitiligoday.org)*

These websites serve as valuable sources of information, support, and community for individuals with vitiligo, helping to increase awareness and understanding of the condition.

As I close this chapter of my life, I am filled with profound gratitude and a sense of awe for the journey I have traveled. My heartfelt thanks go out to all those who have accompanied me on this path, supporting and encouraging me through every triumph and challenge.

To my family, whose unwavering love and acceptance have been my foundation, thank you for seeing the beauty in my uniqueness and reminding me of my worth, no matter the circumstances. Your love has been a guiding light, giving me the strength to embrace my canvas with pride.

To my friends, who have stood by my side and lifted me up during moments of doubt, thank you for your unwavering support and for reminding me that true friendship goes beyond appearances. Your presence has brought joy and laughter to my life, adding vibrant colors to my story.

To the countless individuals I have encountered along the way, whether it was a smile, a kind word, or a gesture of acceptance, thank you for your openness and compassion. Each interaction has left an imprint on my heart, reminding me of the power of human connection and the importance of embracing diversity.

And finally, to those who are reading this book, whether you have vitiligo or not, I extend my deepest gratitude. Thank you for taking the time to explore my journey, to learn and understand. May my story inspire you to embrace your own uniqueness and to see the beauty in the differences that surround us.

As I conclude this book, I leave you with a message: **Embrace the canvas of your life, for it is painted with the hues of your experiences, your challenges, and your triumphs. Embrace the colors that make you who you are, for they are what make you truly beautiful.** And most importantly, embrace others with open hearts and minds, for in celebrating diversity, we create a world where acceptance and love thrive.

With heartfelt gratitude,
Roshaan Narkedayy